The Runaway Train:
A Metaphor of the Plight of African American Children
By Dr. James M. Thompson, I

Illustrated by Lindsey Bailey

The Runaway Train:
A Metaphor of the Plight of African American Children

James M. Thompson, I, Ph.D.
Author

Danna H. Thompson, M.D.
Editor

Lindsey Bailey
Illustrator

First Printing: 2018
ISBN 978-0-692-17501-9

Dr. James M. Thompson, I
PO Box 232
Blythewood, SC 29016

Ordering Information:

Special discounts are available on quantity purchases by corporations, associations, educators, and others. For details, contact the publisher at the above listed address.

U.S. trade bookstores and wholesalers: Please contact Dr. James M. Thompson, I. Tel: (803) 466-4006; email jamathompson@gmail.com.

Dedication

This book is dedicated to God's priceless gifts, my beautiful children sent from heaven above: Jamey, James II, and Jaley.

"Train up a child in the way he should go: and when he is old, he will not depart from it." - Proverbs 22:6 (KJV)

Acknowledgements

First of all, I must give all honor and thanks to my Lord and Savior Jesus Christ for His many blessings and gifts.

To my Mom and Dad, I want to thank you both for instilling in me the core values and morals to become the man that I am today as a son, husband, and father.

I am thankful for a "friend who sticks closer than a brother," Pastor Dr. Kenny W. Rose who always encourages me to see it through until the end.

I have to thank my incredible illustrator, Lindsey Bailey, for seeing my vision and helping me to bring life to this book.

Last but not least, I must thank my helpmate and God sent wife, Danna, for your endless support and helping me to maintain my focus while writing this book. You are more than just an awesome wife. For you are an incredible mother to our three beautiful children. I love you all!

Table of Contents

It is five o'clock and quitting time as I walked out of my downtown high-rise office. I am thankful that I did not have to walk outside in that terrible summer rain storm. I have the luxury of walking through the catwalk linking my office to the parking garage. As I was walking, I couldn't help but say aloud, "Life is great!" realizing that not even a single raindrop will fall on me. Once I leave this parking garage, I will drive straight to suburbia and park in my double car garage. I'm living my best life in my "own world." Suburban America is a privilege for the select few who can make it. So many dream this life that I live, but only a few can attain it. I had to go beyond just dreaming it and instead turn my fantasies into reality. It is no surprise in this reality that very few look like me, but that is how it has to be.

While taking the fastest route home, I have to drive through public housing neighborhoods infested with crimes, drugs, and poverty with the worst public schools in the state that only perpetuates their environment. Police are an ever present force conducting raids. I can't help but think, "You people will never get out of this 'hood!" Funny I should say that considering that it was once my plight. But as I often reflect on my life's journey, I decided that I was going to take the path least traveled to escape that oppressive environment. My mother knew a good education was the only way to create a better reality for her children to get out of these streets. As I passed through my old 'hood, I always see former classmates who were the popular, "cool" kids still living there.

No surprise down the street there were several more officers with a Black male handcuffed and being forced into the backseat of a squad car. I am glad that I don't have to deal with all that unnecessary, low-life, ghetto, and hood rich drama. I am now fortunate enough to be able to retreat to my upper crust little world filled with lush, manicured lawns where next door neighbors don't steal your cable. It is not as if I think I am better than others or trying to be somebody I am not. I just want to live a better life and be able to afford the pleasures of life. Therefore, this is the primary reason I decided to escape the hustle and bustle of that "hood" life.

Finally, I pulled up to the 24 hour security guard gatehouse at the entrance of my exclusive resort style subdivision with amenities, such as an Olympic size swimming pool, a gymnasium with full basketball court, five tennis courts, ten ponds, and a well manicured 18-hole course for the golf enthusiasts. The security guard politely waved at me as he pressed the button to open the gate to my oasis. I proceeded to drive to my humble abode to escape this nasty weather. I enjoy driving home in the evening and admiring my well-lit yard with beautiful landscaping. With just one click, my garage door opened up, and I was finally out of the elements.

As I walked into the comfort of my 5,000 square foot home, with the simple touch of a button I am able to turn on the 84-inch Ultra HD 4K television, custom home entertainment center with stereo surround sound to play my favorite music, and pre-set lights throughout. I worked extremely hard to purchase my mansion as I had to pay my way through college working several part-time jobs. I eventually earned my MBA degree from one of the most prestigious business schools in the country. All my life, I had to pull myself up by the bootstraps in order to make something of myself. I didn't get a handout nor did I expect or ask for a handout. Life was not always easy for me, and it certainly wasn't fair. But, I believe if I can make it then anybody should be able to make it in this race called life. I just don't understand why those people I always pass on the way home choose to live in public housing or choose to be on street corners asking for handouts with their tattered cardboard signs depicting their unfortunate plight. Everybody has choices in life; but, they clearly made the worst choices.

BREAKING NEWS! BRE████████S! BREAKIN

After making myself more comfortable, I proceeded to the kitchen to prepare a quick bite to eat when all of a sudden the local news station had a breaking news alert regarding a train that was out of control because its brakes were inoperable. It was also reported that the train was transporting an explosive substance that could ignite upon impact and wipe out an entire town within a 2-mile radius. I really did not give much thought to the breaking news because the train was approximately 100 miles northeast of my town so it was not a direct threat to me. In fact that reminds me of the time when our town recently had a train to derail on Main Street causing a major traffic jam for several hours. No injury was reported in that particular incident.

Well, I continued preparing dinner and was about to sit down when the anchorman reappeared across my screen. "Ahhhhh, man!" I shouted. Now, this is really aggravating me because it's interrupting my favorite television show.

According to the latest report, the train was traveling at only 15 miles per hour but highly explosive. As I thought to myself, "why haven't those people stopped the train and quit making such a big deal about the situation?" I am sure that through the advancement of technology, they could come up with some type of ingenious solution to prevent a major crisis.

The anchorman informed viewers that there is a helicopter flying above the train with a cameraman on board. As I looked at the sky view, I noticed that the conductor was standing at the edge of the train as if he wanted to jump. All of a sudden, the conductor jumped into a grassy field abandoning the train. In fact, as it turns out, the conductor bailed out in order to save his very own life as he believed there was no hope for the runaway train.

Shortly thereafter, a field reporter interviewed the conductor of the abandoned train. The reporter asked "So, Mr. Wilson, can you provide the viewers at home with your account of the malfunctioning train?" Mr. Wilson replied, "Sure. I inspected the train this morning prior to making my routine commute to Caresville, when I detected a minor problem with the brakes to what appeared to be a few worn out parts. I thought to myself that it should not be too bad, and the commute to and fro would not be impossible. So, I left the station at approximately 8 o'clock this morning, and when I applied the brakes to make my first stop I could smell a burning odor and saw small sparks coming from the bottom of the train. What do you know, the train was fine, and I was able to make my first drop off."

The reporter seemed somewhat perplexed due to the early detection of the mechanical problems and asked "Did you think of getting the train repaired at your first stop after making the initial drop off?" The conductor replied, "No, I did not think for one second of getting any repairs done. I have a job to do, and it is not my responsibility to have to inspect and report mechanical issues. That is the locomotive mechanic department's responsibility. I was told from higher up that everyone must stay in their lanes in order for the company to run smoothly. Not only that, I had to make several other drop offs before returning to the station by 3:30 PM when I usually get off. They don't pay me overtime and I am not willing to stay beyond 3:30. Do you know what I mean?"

LIVE

KING NEWS! BREAKING NEWS! BREA

At this point in the interview, the reporter had enough and stated "Thank you for your time, Mr. Wilson! I am, Bill Collins, with WKRK, reporting live at Farmville, now back to you in the studio Addison Moore.

As the train continued to travel, the anchorman was keeping the viewers abreast of the current situation and had a safety inspector on the phone for a live interview. Through the interview, the inspector stated that he was fully aware that the brakes were deteriorating but was waiting for the correct part to arrive to the station for repairs. The anchorman then asked him, "Why did you allow for the train to leave the station if you were aware of the situation?" The inspector replied, "I figured we had a job to do, and the train was half way decent to make the necessary drop offs to meet the deadline. Also, it is really not my fault if that's what you're thinking, because I don't purchase the train parts. The procurement department has been dragging their feet lately and holding up our department from making any progress for weeks now."

At this point, the anchorman was somewhat speechless after listening to the conductor's and safety inspector's perspectives. After the interviews, the anchorman stated that he would keep the viewers informed of any new changes, and we could return to our regular scheduled broadcast. "Finally!" I hollered at the top of my lungs. I really didn't want to see or hear about another train since I already missed half the season finale of my show.

After a fairly relaxing evening and a scrumptious meal, I decided to close my eyes and call it a night.

Author's Train of Thought

The premise of this book is to set the scene that leads to the struggles African American children face using metaphors. Since there are many difficult issues plaguing African American children, I wanted to shed light on the situation in a non-threatening and non-accusatory manner. The intent of this book is not to cast blame by pointing fingers or airing anyone's dirty laundry. Rather, the intent is for individuals who have any type of interactions with African American children to be able to have candid dialogues on what can be done to better serve this population of youth within our schools and communities. Therefore, this book is a tool that will help you to reflect on the many obstacles that African American children are faced with on a daily basis.

It is not enough just to recognize that there are many obstacles before this group of children or even that this group can be somewhat challenging. In order to develop solutions, one must be able to recognize and call the issue what it is in order to produce positive results. It does take an entire village to raise our African American children. Parents cannot do it alone. Grandparents cannot do it alone. Churches cannot do it alone. Community centers cannot do it alone. Mentors cannot do it alone. Teachers cannot do it alone. Schools cannot do it alone. You get the picture! It takes an "entire village," an "entire community," or even an "entire neighborhood" to help bring African American children into adulthood to reach the fullest potential and become productive members of their community.

Yes, I am of the mindset that the first teachers in children's lives should be their parents. But, since I am a realist, I have accepted the fact that we have many parents who choose to be their children's friends as opposed to being their parents. As parents, you have the key responsibility to instill core values and morals into your children. All parents should want more for their children and do everything possible to ensure that life is a little easier for their children than it has been for them.

As you read through the book, it is my hope that individuals will reflect on the struggles that they see on a daily basis. With that being said, there should be a plan of action to move African American children into a positive direction. It is my desire that African American children will be able to see that there are caring adults willing and capable of helping them. If you are parents of African American children, it is critical that you are raising your own children and not expecting that vital role to be filled by others.

"All Aboard!" (Reflection)

As you peruse *The Runaway Train: A Metaphor of the Plight of African American Children*, there are various characters mentioned throughout the book. Now, it is your turn to "Get on Board" as you reflect on the significance of each character. The following page contains questions that you can use as a reflection or even for a group discussion.

Expectations: Have an open-mind and be willing to view things from different perspectives. Don't take everything too personal. Realize that we exist in a diverse community and not in a vacuum. Set aside your beliefs and preconceived notions of your thoughts toward African American children. Lastly, avoid just being a complainer and develop a plan of action to do something positive to help the situation.

Guided Questions

Which one character can you mostly relate to and why?

Which character(s) remind you of someone you know and how?

What does it mean to "pull oneself up by the bootstraps?" Is this a good or bad thing? Explain.

What is your opinion of the successful African American man who believes it is the responsibilities of other people to stop the runaway train?

What can you infer of the successful African American man's following thought: "I am glad that I don't have to deal with all that unnecessary, low-life, ghetto, and hood rich drama because I am fortunate enough to be able to retreat to my upper crust little world."

Often time, two worlds exist between the "haves" and "have nots." Why did the author describe the two distinct worlds?

The author mentioned "this race called life." Describe "this race called life" in terms of why there are gaps or disparities when it comes to salary, educational attainment, home ownership, bank lending, entrepreneurship, as the list continues between African Americans and other subgroups in the United States of America.

What person in the story should be held responsible for the inoperable brakes on the train? Why?

Explain the reasoning behind the metaphor of African American children as the runaway train carrying explosives. Be sure to identify some of the explosives, i.e., struggles, obstacles, and challenges.

What measures could have been in place to have prevented the train from becoming inoperable in the first place?

The conductor bailed out of the train because "he believed there was no hope." In real life, who is really the "conductor" that bailed out on the African American children's lives because "he [or she] believed there was no hope?"

Predict the outcome of the runaway train and explain your stance.

About the Author

Dr. James M. Thompson serves as an associate minister at United Bible Way Church of Lancaster under the pastoral leadership of Pastor Dr. Kenny W. Rose since 2007. Dr. Thompson is an assistant principal of curriculum and instruction at Hand Middle School in Richland County School District One in Columbia, South Carolina

He has held several positions in K-12 education since 2002. He served as a seventh grade science teacher, Advanced Placement Teacher Specialist, a science and health instructor at an alternative school, and GEAR UP Project Director.

Dr. Thompson has authored and received grants that funded many school- and community-based initiatives totaling over $500,000. Among other selected honors and awards, he was named Beginning Teacher of the Year; selected as a White House Fellowship Regional Finalist; inducted into Phi Kappa Phi Honor Society; named to Who's Who Among America's Teachers; named Omega Man of the Year through the Kappa Pi Chapter of Omega Psi Phi Fraternity, Inc.; and a South Carolina Education Policy Fellow. Currently, he has been accepted into the Center for Executive Education Leadership's Aspiring Principals Cohort and the South Carolina Department of Education Building Instructional Capacity Cohort.

Dr. Thompson has earned five (5) college degrees: a Bachelor of Science degree in biology with a minor in psychology from The University of South Carolina; a Master of Arts in Health Services Management and a Master of Business Administration from Webster University; an Educational Specialist degree in Educational Administration and a Doctor of Philosophy degree in Educational Administration with dual minors, in (1) research and statistics and (2) instructional technology from The University of Southern Mississippi.

Dr. Thompson enjoys spending quality time with his family, reading motivational books, furthering his education, and being a servant leader. He also spends time talking with his best friends and beloved mentors, his parents. He is married to a God-fearing woman, Dr. Danna H. Thompson. From their blissful union, they are the proud parents of three beautiful children.

www.ingramcontent.com/pod-product-compliance
Lightning Source LLC
Chambersburg PA
CBHW040252100426
42811CB00011B/1239